ECONOMI

SURVIVING GLOBAL CURRENCY COLLAPSE

SAFEGUARD YOUR FINANCIAL FUTURE WITH SILVER AND GOLD

ALEX NKENCHOR UWAJEH

Legal Disclaimers

This book is presented to you for informational purposes only and is not a substitution for any professional advice. The contents herein are based on the views and opinions of the author and all associated contributors.

While every effort has been made by the author and all associated contributors to present accurate and up to date information within this document, it is apparent technologies rapidly change. Therefore, the author and all associated contributors reserve the right to update the contents and information provided herein as these changes progress. The author and/or all associated contributors take no responsibility for any errors or omissions if such discrepancies exist within this document.

The author and all other contributors accept no responsibility for any consequential actions taken, whether monetary, legal, or otherwise, by any and all readers of the materials provided. It is the reader's sole responsibility to seek professional advice before taking any action on their part.

Readers results will vary based on their skill level and individual perception of the contents herein, and thus no guarantees, monetarily or otherwise, can be made accurately. Therefore, no guarantees are made.

Discount available for bulk buying

email: sales@247BroadStreet.com

All glory and honour to God for insight and wisdom.

Table of Contents

Contents

Global Currency Collapse

In the event of global currency collapse, if there is no other currency available to take on the role of money, then it is likely the world will fall back on bartering to obtain the goods they need. In such a situation, it's hard to talk about capital preservation, as most people will be more interested in finding a way to feed their families and make sure they have shelter.

It might sound completely ludicrous but a currency collapse on a global level would lead to more than civil and social unrest. Once things settled down, it would still likely take a long time for people to learn to trust fiat currency again, which is why bartering will become the name of the game.

You have food and your neighbour has gas so you barter, agreeing on what would be considered a fair price. It is likely that gold and silver will start being used more and

more often, as they have intrinsic value and have been used as money throughout the ages. So, it wouldn't be long before gold and silver become the standard currency, which is why it is so important that everyone safeguards their future by converting as many of their assets as possible into gold and silver.

Of course, this isn't to say you should convert your entire portfolio into precious metals. The risk of global currency collapse is present but there is no guarantee it will happen. And while investing in gold and silver is a good idea and certainly not a losing trade, it's also an investment likely to make substantial gains. Many investors choose to keep approximately one third of their portfolio in higher-risk and higher-gain investment with the remaining two thirds allocated to medium and low risk investments.

If you are risk adverse, your percentages might differ somewhat. However, the key is that you should be allocating a hefty portion of your portfolio to gold and silver. And regardless of the type of investment, it's probably a wise idea to buy physical gold and silver. Irrespective of what happens, whether it's worldwide currency collapse or all-out war, if you own physical gold and silver, it can always be traded for things you need.

Once currency collapses, the majority of your paper investments, including stocks, futures, options and so on and so forth, become virtually useless. This is why you need to make sure that you have plenty of gold in your portfolio and not just ETFs or mining stocks.

The Gold Standard vs Fiat Paper Currency

Gold coins have been used as money for thousands of years but there were problems with using gold as currency. This was because for normal trade, gold coins were too valuable to be used. In fact, they were mainly used by the wealthy for certain types of transactions, including paying taxes and business.

Eventually, as a solution so people didn't carry around vast amounts of wealth on them, paper currency was invented. Remember that prices were very different and one gold coin could buy you a few acres of land, so you can imagine how dangerous it could be carrying around so much wealth.

Paper money gradually came about, though there were various different other forms of currency used in lieu of gold, such as sticks with notches representing certain amounts

of gold. Regardless of the type of currency, the common thing they all had was they were all based on gold. This eventually became known as the gold standard.

Historically speaking, the gold standard worked for a very long time and during that period, you could theoretically exchange a paper banknote for gold and the bank was obligated to give you the equivalent in gold. However, it was rarely practiced.

The way it worked was that people would deposit their gold coins in the bank's vault and receive paper currency in exchange. This paper money caught on quite quickly because it was easier to carry around, so it was definitely a lot more practical, and it was easier to break up the value of a coin into multiple notes, making it easier to trade.

Slowly, over the years, the gold standard evolved into the concept we know today, whereby a country couldn't issue more paper currency than the amount of gold in its reserves. It also meant that exchange rates were stable because many countries' currencies were valued against the price of gold.

However, there were problems with this because the price of gold tended to fluctuate just as it does now. In other words, if there was panic in the market or production was lower than expected, prices of gold would soar, which would lead to inflation. Conversely, when prices of gold would drop due to new gold veins being discovered, increased production or a booming economy, the market would suffer from deflation.

While the gold standard may not have been perfect, it did stop governments and central banks from manipulating the value of currency as they saw fit. The moment the

gold standard was abolished, governments and central banks had the power to print money as they saw fit. They were no longer bound by any rules and regulations.

The problem with being able to issue money whenever one chooses is that the value of fiat currency is determined by a few factors, including supply and demand as well as the population's faith in that currency. Thus, the more fiat money is printed, the lower the value of one unit, in other words the fewer goods you can purchase for one unit of currency. An excess of currency can lead to hyperinflation and even a complete collapse of the value of paper money.

Fiat currency refers to any form of paper money that isn't tied to gold and its value is derived from the fact that the population accepts it as money and has faith in the government, which accepts payment in this form.

Now, the question arises regarding which option is better. Would the gold standard be preferable to the current fiat currency system? Many say no, because the price of gold cannot be controlled whereas the value of fiat currency can. This is true because a central bank can withdraw paper currency from the market and stabilize inflation or increase the supply to prevent deflation.

However, there is another problem that many don't realize. Many central banks are privately owned by large financial groups. And these financial groups aren't interested in ensuring people have a good lifestyle, which would mean balancing the supply of fiat currency to avoid inflation. They are interested in making money.

Take the Federal Reserve Bank as an example. The Fed is in charge of issuing currency. However, instead of just "handing" the money over to the

government, they charge interest. Thus, practically, the government is forced to borrow money from its own central bank.

So, take the stimulus packages the US government used to attempt to restart the economy after the crash in 2008. Logically, you would think the best course of action would be to print more money to cover the debt, right? Well, that's not quite accurate.

Firstly, an increase in supply of paper currency leads to the devaluation of that currency. Secondly, since the government is practically borrowing from the Fed, it has to pay interest, which means an increase in the deficit. So, they'd have to print even more money to try and cover the deficit. However, the more they print, the more it will cost them and the less the dollar is worth. It's a vicious cycle that can lead to the complete collapse of paper currency.

Note that this is happening in much of Europe as well and in most western countries. Thus, it's not strictly relegated to the US.

So, does that mean the gold standard is a better option? It could be but just like the fiat currency system, it will only work if it's properly regulated. Remember, gold itself has value because people believe it does. It doesn't feed you or keep you warm. It's a piece of metal that's used in industrial applications and for jewelry mainly, so its real value comes from the fact that we believe it's valuable. Just like with paper currency.

So, either system can work effectively as long as there are proper rules and regulations in place. But this type of regulatory framework has to be established by a government that isn't being lobbied by private corporations every minute of the day

and isn't worried about re-election but about sorting out the monetary system.

The main problem is that things will have to get a lot worse before they get better, because people have been used to living on debt for much too long, which is the main problem. You would think that the recent financial catastrophe would have taught us a lesson. It worked for about a year – maybe – but then people reverted to borrowing significant amounts and now, things are almost as bad in terms of individual debt levels as they were pre-crisis.

Central Banks and Bullion Gold

One thing is certain. When central banks start buying up gold, you have to wonder what's coming. These are the same people who, not long ago, claimed that gold was nothing more than a relic, a throwback to a different era and that those who sought it

out as a hedge for their wealth were living in the past. They even sold off as much of their gold as they could, causing the price to plummet.

After such statements and actions, you wouldn't expect central banks to start buying up gold like it was going out of fashion. According to a report released by the World Gold Council on the 2011 gold market, overall investment in gold increased by a mere 5%. However, the volume of gold central banks bought increased by approximately 500% from 2010, a year which also showed a significant increase in central banks' appetite for gold.

So, what does this all mean? After all, they sold off all their gold, causing the price of gold to tank because of the massive supply that was suddenly available. And now they are buying it up at five or six times the price.

These are the people who convinced governments to abandon the gold standard to switch to fiat currencies, which they could only obtain from central banks at a cost. In other words, every unit of money printed brought debt along with it.

And now? central banks find themselves in the situation in which they are printing money for governments that can't afford to pay their debts. In other words, paper currency is slowly but surely heading downhill and soon it won't be worth the paper it's printed on.

What's even worse is that by buying up all this gold, they are further devaluing paper currency due to the message they are sending. Why should people store their savings in dollars, euros, yen or any other paper currency, when banks are converting their fiat money into gold?

So, essentially, it's a vicious cycle because central banks are sending out the message that they don't have faith in their own creation. It probably won't be long before we see a complete collapse of global currencies. At least that's what we can conclude from the fact that central banks purchased 440 tons of gold in 2011 versus 77 tons in 2010.

Gold vs. Silver

So, why is everyone so set on gold and silver? Why do all traders and investors seem to throw their money at gold and silver the moment they sense something might be wrong with the market?

The answers are quite simple. Gold and silver are considered precious metals and have been favoured by investors for a very long time as they maintain their inherent value, regardless of the state of the economy. Silver and gold are prized and

rare metals. In the history of time they each have held their trading value well.

Of course, gold has always been the more valuable of the two precious metals but that is due to some of its unique properties as well as the fact that it is quite a bit rarer than silver.

Gold and Silver to Safeguard Your Financial Future

Clearly, investing in silver and gold will help protect your assets in the event of a worldwide currency collapse. While many people claim this can't happen, there are just as many signs pointing to it as a serious possibility. If global currency collapse does occur, you will need to have some form of wealth protection in place that not only ensures you are protecting the value of your assets but can also be converted into everyday items you will need.

In a situation in which all currencies across the globe have crashed, other markets will follow, starting with the stock market. The only things that will have true value are commodities. However, you will need to have a way to trade them, which is why it is a good idea to have physical gold stored in an easily accessible place.

Note that keeping everything in the bank might seem like a good idea but if currencies do crash, it won't be a pretty sight. People will see their life savings vanish in an instant. They will realize the money in their wallets can't even buy them a loaf of bread and they are no longer able to feed their families. This will lead to social unrest. So, you are better off keeping your physical gold in a safe location known to yourself only to ensure easy access in order to purchase goods required for the survival of your family.

Of course, even if the decline is more gradual and doesn't necessarily lead to social unrest, people will still likely switch over to using gold and silver as money because they will have more faith in a metal that has always maintained its value compared to paper money.

Thus, it's wise to have a relatively good portion of your investment portfolio allotted to gold and silver. You also might consider varying the types of investments you make. For example, when you invest in gold, you aren't limited to physical gold. There are many other options, including futures, gold exchange traded funds and more.

The mix you choose depends on your appetite for risk and the main reason you are investing in gold or silver. If you are looking to simply preserve your capital, then you probably want a solution that doesn't involve too much risk and that would

generally be to invest in physical gold or silver. On the other hand, if you aren't averse to a bit of risk and are looking for growth, then maybe gold futures or options are a better choice, especially if you don't wish to invest too much of your own capital.

So, there are essentially three objectives when it comes to investing in this particular asset class and depending on which you choose, that will determine the type of vehicles you will use to invest.

Thus, one objective to invest in gold and silver, which is completely different from any other asset class, is for capital preservation. This is the most common goal among investors when they invest in precious metals. Basically, the idea is to protect their assets from currency devaluation. While there's nothing wrong with making a profit, in this case most investors are more interested in protecting what they already have and maintaining the value of their assets rather than making a profit.

However, most people are after capital appreciation when they invest in gold and silver, it doesn't mean you can't also profit from these precious metals. Thus, if your goal is capital appreciation, there are a few tactics you can employ. First of all, you can speculate by buying the metals at a low price and selling them at a high price and hope to make a good profit in the interim. If you're looking for something more long term, you could invest in gold or silver when the prices are down – or the economy is booming – and sell when the prices are up – which is during a recession. This can take years but the profits are well worth the delay.

You can also invest in gold and silver to create a new income stream for yourself.

This can be done either through trading, which can net you some nice profits if you know what you are doing or through dividend investing. The latter means that instead of you purchasing physical gold, you would purchase dividend stocks in a mining company. This would allow you to have the exposure you want on gold but still earn an annual income from the dividends.

Dividend investing is an excellent way to grow what you already have because the money you earn can be reinvested into more equity. The result is more shares and higher dividends.

Regardless of what your main objective is and how you structure your investment portfolio, it's still a good idea to ensure that you own some physical gold as well. While stocks, futures and options might look great on paper, if currencies crash, they become worthless.

Factors Affecting the Price
of Gold and Silver

There are many things that have an impact on the prices of gold and silver but the more you understand about these precious metals and what makes them tick, the better your chances are of making the right investment decisions.

So, first and foremost, we have market sentiment. This is what many traders and investors forget, especially when they sit and stare at charts all day long. The market is comprised of human beings making human decisions. These decisions are not always logical nor are they necessarily right but human emotion will always play a part in the markets. This is why market sentiment is so important.

For example, let's presume that the economy seems to be going all right. Everything seems positive and, in fact, it

actually is. However, someone has a different agenda and they launch a rumour saying a big bank is about to go under. The rumour is generally enough for people to withdraw their life savings and convert them into gold and silver. The result is that it drives up the price of gold and silver.

Historically speaking, if you look at the price of gold, during the economic boom it was relatively low since no one wanted to buy into gold. It was seen as a waste of time because it couldn't provide capital appreciation and who needed capital preservations during a boom.

However, things changed and suddenly, gold and silver became the most important investments possible because people couldn't believe what they were seeing. These companies and banks were too big to fail, weren't they? Unfortunately, no, they weren't. And as a result people turned to

gold right away to protect themselves from a very uncertain future. After all, who knew what could happen?

Sadly, we find ourselves in much the same situation. We know something is going to happen and we doubt it's a good thing. It could be the collapse of global currencies or it could be a serious recession, bigger than the last one. And this is why many people are turning to gold, going on the principle that it's better to be safe than to be sorry, which is quite accurate.

Another factor that influences the price of gold and silver is, obviously, currency. The weaker the dollar is, for example, the higher the value of gold, when it comes to silver, supply and demand has an important impact on price. However, with gold, things differ. Gold doesn't move so significantly in terms of supply and demand because of the various stockpiles. It is well known that

banks can influence the price of gold by withholding or releasing their reserves. For this reason, the market doesn't take much notice of supply and demand levels.

The value of currency, however, plays a much bigger role. The lower the value of currency, the more people will turn to gold to hedge their investments against inflation and complete currency collapse.

Fiscal and interest rate policies also have an influence on the price of gold and silver. The lower the interest rate is, the more people will be interested in purchasing commodities such as precious metals. If the interest rate is high, on the other hand, people tend to shift towards less risky alternatives, such as treasury bills and deposits. Otherwise, it would be very difficult to make a profit.

During economic growth, central banks raised interest rates to make credit more expensive. This way, they kept inflation

under control. Unfortunately, the high interest rates also made it that no one was interested in precious metals because their growth potential was practically non-existent.

In terms of fiscal policies, the more currency a government decides to print and release into the economy, the lower the value of one unit of that currency will be. Thus, the more currency is printed, the higher the price of gold as more and more people turn to it to protect their assets.

Another factor that dictates the price of precious metals is the extraction and production process. Gold mining is becoming increasingly expensive and the rise in production costs as well as currency devaluation has all had an impact on the price of gold. There is less and less gold being produced every year because there isn't much gold left in areas that are easy to

get to. Any new gold that has been found over the past few years has been in areas that are extremely difficult to mine.

Bureaucracy can also be an issue because getting mining permits can take as long as a decade, which, of course, drives up the price of gold. Then there are the price increases of all the other resources needed to mine gold, which also affect the price of gold itself by making it more expensive to mine.

Precious Metals: A Hedge for the Big Boys

The price of gold has gone up significantly because more and more large organizations are turning to gold to hedge their assets. As a result of the financial meltdown, many banks and financial institutions came to the realization that they needed to expand their portfolios and preferably with something tangible, hence so many turned to

commodities. However, many chose the low-risk path of capital preservation and invested in gold. After all, why go through such a complicated problem again when one has the choice of being protected.

Thus, most companies chose to invest in gold in such a way that they could have access to the physical product rather than investing in paper alone. The liquidity of physical gold can't really be matched and, in the worst scenario, it can be traded for goods and services, even if currencies

collapse completely.

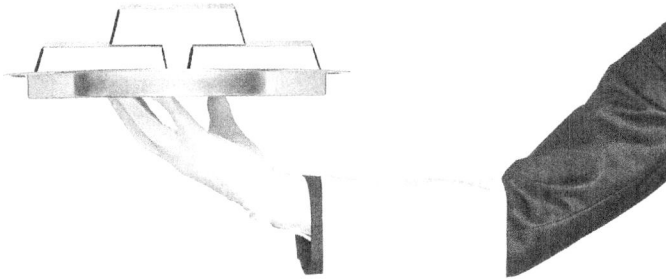

Gold and Silver Investment Vehicles

So, now that you have a good idea of why you should invest in gold and silver and what drives the price of these precious metals, it's time to look at how you can invest in them.

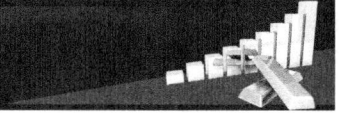

There are a number of ways you can invest in gold and silver. You can either own it physically by purchasing coins or bullion or you can limit yourself to exposure to price fluctuations by investing in mining stocks, ETF and other financial instruments. The choice is yours but if you are looking to safeguard your financial future against global currency collapse, the best option will likely be to turn to physical gold and silver as it is more likely to maintain its value and is more liquid. Thus, it is easier to trade for the goods you might need, whereas stocks will become practically worthless in such a situation.

Investment Gold and Silver Bullion Coins

One great thing about purchasing gold bullion coins is that you can gain exposure to physical gold without having to make massive investments. You don't need to buy

tons of it to still have a decent level of capital preservation. It also doesn't hurt that you can change over gradually, buying small amounts at a time, until you reach a level you are pleased with. Note, that quite a few countries do not charge Value Added Tax on gold bullion coins, which doesn't hurt at all.

When it comes to gold bullion coins, you have lots of options because there are lots of countries that issue gold bullion coins. When it comes to the global market value of these coins, it is usually calculated according to the amount of gold included in the coin and a premium. On the other hand, in the country where they are minted, these coins are usually valued at the face value stamped on them.

The premium on gold coins varies according to a number of factors but the size of the coin plays a significant role as well. The

smaller the coin, the higher the production cost, which means the premium will be higher. Note that the premium also includes the dealer's commission.

The same applies to silver bullion coins except that they have one major advantage over gold, namely that they are cheaper though silver maintains its value just like gold. In fact, many retail investors prefer silver over gold because the entry barrier is much lower. For example, the average price of gold was $1,571.52 per ounce in 2011, while the average price of silver was $35.12, which was considered a record high.

So, as you can imagine, it's much easier to start stocking up on silver than gold yet one can enjoy a similar degree of capital preservation.

Let's look at some of the more popular gold and silver coins.

Australian Gold Nugget and Gold Lunar Bullion Coins:

The Australian Gold Nugget is a gold bullion coin minted by the Perth Mint. They are produced in denominations of 1/20 oz, 1/10 oz, ¼ oz, ½ oz, 1 oz, 2 oz, 10 oz and 1 kg. In other words, there's an Australian Gold Nugget that contains 1 kg of pure, 24k gold.

These coins have legal tender status in Australia and, surprisingly, they get a design makeover every year. Due to the fact that only a limited number of these coins are produced every year, these coins tend to have a higher value than just that of the gold content they include. However, regardless of the design, the coins always feature a kangaroo. They are also referred to as Gold Kangaroos.

The Australian Lunar coins are similar to the Gold Kangaroo or Gold Nugget in terms of denominations and gold content. The only real difference lies in the images minted on the coins. Instead of using the popular kangaroo, these coins feature images of different animals from the Chinese calendar.

Australian Kangaroo and Kookaburra Silver Bullion Coins

Like its gold counterpart, the Australian Silver Kangaroo is a silver bullion coin minted by the Perth Mint and despite the fact that every year it is redesigned, it always feature a kangaroo.

This silver bullion coin weighs one troy ounce, in compliance with international standards, which is the equivalent of 31.1 grams. It has a purity of 99.9% and a face value of $1 Australian dollar. While the coin is considered legal tender, it's not meant to be circulated.

The Australian Silver Kookaburra is considered to be the most popular Australian silver bullion coins. This is mainly due to their design, since it changes constantly, featuring a different image on the reverse of the coin. While many other silver bullion coins are available in sizes of one troy ounce and fractional sizes such as ½ ounce coins, the Silver Kookaburra is only available as a 1 ounce, 2 ounce, 10 ounce and 1 kilogram coin.

Australian Lunar and Koala Silver Bullion Coins

The Australian Silver Lunar coin features images based on the progression of the Chinese zodiac, which makes it a highly desirable coin for collectors. Thus, every year a Silver Lunar coin is minted in accordance with the Chinese zodiac, featuring the respective animal. For

example, 2011 was the Year of the Rabbit and a rabbit was featured on the coin.

The Australian Silver Koala is a relatively new silver bullion coin as it was first minted in 2007. It features a koala, as you would expect. It is available as a one ounce, 10 ounce and 1 kilogram coin.

Austrian Philharmonic Gold Bullion Coins

The Austrian Philharmonic is one of the most popular gold coins in Europe. In fact, in 2008 it was the most popular in the world, as the 1oz denomination sold more units than U.S. Eagles or Krugerrands. This coin is minted in one-ounce, half-ounce, quarter ounce and one tenth ounces.

Austrian Silver Vienna Philharmonic Coin

The Austrian Silver Vienna Philharmonic is a silver bullion coin that is practically identical

in design with its gold counterpart. It was first minted in 2008 and has a purity of 99.9% silver. They are highly popular due to the exquisite design, being considered the most beautiful silver bullion coins in Europe.

Canadian Maple Leaf

The Canadian Maple Leaf was first minted in 1979 and represented Canada's entry into the competitive gold bullion market. It is minted in one-ounce, half an ounce, quarter of an ounce and one tenth ounce sizes. In 2008, due to the financial crisis, the sale of these coins increased dramatically as people struggled to protect their assets. Thus, instead of 278,600 ounces being sold, which was the number for 2007, in 2008 896,000 ounces were sold, making for more than triple the sales.

Canadian Silver Maple Leaf

The Canadian Silver Maple Leaf is a silver bullion coin that was first minted in 1988 by the Royal Canadian Mint. It features a 99.99% level of purity, marking it as the silver bullion coin with the highest degree of silver purity in the world. The coin usually has a maple leaf on it.

Chinese Panda Gold Bullion Coins

The Chinese Panda differs from other gold coins in two main ways. First of all, the Panda design on the back of the coin changes every year and, secondly, each coin is minted as a limited edition. These coins are minted in 1 oz, ½ oz, ¼ oz and 1/10 oz and 1/20 oz denominations. This gold bullion coin was first introduced in 1982.

Chinese Panda Silver Bullion Coins

The Chinese Silver Panda was first minted in 1983 and every year it has featured a different panda design. This often makes it more expensive than other silver bullion coins due to higher premiums. This silver bullion coin contains 1 troy ounce of silver and has a purity of 99.9%.

South African Krugerrand Gold Bullion Coins

The South African Krugerrand was first minted in 1967. The idea was to help market and export gold from South Africa. The coin became quite popular and, surprisingly, by 1980 it represented 90% of the market in terms of gold coins in the world.

The South African Krugerrand actually served as the inspiration for many other

countries to mint their own coins, including Canada, Australia, the U.S. and the U.K.

United Kingdom Britannia Gold Bullion Coins

The Britannia coins are British gold bullion coins issued by the Royal Mint. The gold coins date back to 1987. In 1997, a silver version went into production.

Gold Britannia coins are minted in one ounce, half ounce, quarter ounce and tenth ounce denominations.

United Kingdom Silver Bullion Coins

Silver Britannia coins are a highly popular silver bullion coin but only feature a 95.84% degree of silver purity, which is surprising as it makes it the least pure coin on the market. However, it should be noted that each coin still contains one troy ounce of silver, except that the actual weight of the coin is higher due to the lower purity. It has

a face value of £2 but its current market value exceeds £30.

USA - Buffalo and American Eagle

The American Gold Eagle is the official gold bullion coin of the United States and was first released in 1986. It is authorized under the Gold Bullion Coin Act of 1985 and is available in 1/10 oz, ¼ oz, ½ oz and 1 oz denominations. The gold purity of the coins is 22 karat and, by law, the gold used in these coins must come from America. There are also silver and platinum versions of this coin.

The American Buffalo was first minted in 2006 and is the first time a pure gold bullion coin of 24k was minted by the United States government.

USA - American Silver Eagle

The American Silver Eagle was first minted in 1986 and is considered the official silver

bullion coin of the United States. It is available as a one-ounce coin with a 99.9% degree of silver purity.

Regardless of the type of coin you choose to purchase, remember that you will pay a larger premium for smaller coins. Additionally, consider that it might be a better idea to purchase bars since they come with a smaller premium. The production system isn't quite as complicated as it is with coins.

Gold and Silver Bars

Gold bars are another excellent way one can invest in physical gold. In fact, sometimes they are the better option because they don't carry such a high premium compared to coins. Another advantage is that there are so many different bars available in terms of size that the choice is practically limitless. This makes it easy for anyone to invest in gold.

Note that the purity of the gold content in bars is generally around 99.5% but it can differ. Gold bars are used significantly in the jewelry and industrial sectors but are often preferred by investors because of the low entry barrier. The smaller the gold bar, the cheaper it is to purchase.

In terms of silver, many prefer silver bullion bars since they are easy to store due to their rectangular shape. Like gold, they are available in a wide range of sizes, starting at 1 oz bar going all the way up to 1,000 oz bars, which weigh about 31 kg. Note that silver bars have a purity of 99.9%.

A highly popular silver bar for investment is the 100 oz bar, which weighs 3.11 kg. Its popularity stems from the fact that it features a lower premium than one would have to pay for purchasing 100 bars weighing one ounce or 10 bars weighing ten ounces. This bar makes sense for the retail

investor because one can save money on premiums while still making a reasonable investment.

Storing Silver and Gold

Once you've started investing in silver and gold bullion, you'll face a logistical issue, namely where and how to store your investment. There are a few options and each carries its own advantages and disadvantages. Thus, you can store the bullion yourself or allow a third party to hold it for you.

Storing the Bullion Yourself

If you don't have a large quantity of bullion, whether it's silver or gold, you have the option of storing it at home. Of course, you will have to find a secure place for it, like a safe or some other concealed location.

Some people think burying their bullion is a good way to protect it from being stolen, as

many did during the Great Depression, but this isn't exactly the best course of action. First of all, when it comes to silver, it is highly corrosive and it should be handled as little as possible. Burying it in the ground will only devalue the silver content. The longer it stays in the ground, the more money you lose.

Let's not forget that many people have buried their precious metals only to forget where they buried them. This was a common problem for people during the Great Depression as they buried cash and bullion to keep it from being confiscated by the government only to forget where it was buried. Then, some lucky homeowner who purchased the property years later made a stunning discovery.

While storing your bullion at home is not the most advisable course of action, if you do decide to go down this route, you should

take some precautions. Firstly, don't store all your fortune in one place. If you do get robbed, at least you have a chance of saving some of your bullion this way.

Of course, you want to ensure you conceal it as well as possible but you also have to remember where you hid it. Additionally, make sure you don't tell anyone about the bullion in your home, including your friends. You never know what they might let slip and to whom, which could make you target of thieves.

Storing Your Bullion in a Safety Deposit Box

A better option is to store your bullion in a safety deposit box at a reputable bank. However, it is imperative that you only store your gold or silver with a bank that is financially sound because if they do become insolvent, you risk being unable to access

your safety deposit box because you simply wouldn't be able to get into the bank.

There are also other drawbacks, including the potential failure of the world banking system or even the government deciding to confiscate physical gold, which would not be a first. Note, though, that there are some countries where this is less likely to happen so if you have a large amount of gold, you might want to opt for a safety deposit box overseas.

When deciding which bank to store your bullion in, you need to take a good look at the bank's results. If it has a history of weathering financial storms well, then it's a good bet your bullion will be safe.

Storing Your Investment with a Bullion Dealer

Many bullion dealers not only sell silver and gold bullion but also provide storage

services in exchange for a fee. This is often a good choice because it is safer than storing it at home and it's also easier to turn your gold or silver into cash if necessary. Additionally, there is less risk because there is no transportation required.

Note that some bullion companies will offer insurance within the fee while with others, you will have to take out a policy yourself.

Allocated Storage

Another option you have is to invest in bullion with a bank and opt for allocated storage. In this case, you own the metal – most commonly gold - but like with a bullion dealer, you don't take possession of it. The bank stores it in its vaults. Since it is your property, the bullion is safe if the bank becomes insolvent.

However, there is a drawback in that access can be difficult if this does occur. Therefore,

you want to make sure you choose a bank that has a good financial history and isn't likely to fail in the event of another crash.

Keep in mind, though, that the fees for allocated storage can be quite high as most banks want to encourage people to invest in bullion using unallocated storage.

Unallocated Storage

Unallocated storage is probably the worst option for any investor, even though banks will generally try and sell it to you as being the best way to invest in bullion. When you buy bullion and opt for unallocated storage, you actually don't own the metal itself. Instead, you are actually receiving a promise that you will be supplied with x amount of gold or silver when you request it. Practically, you are lending the bank money.

The biggest disadvantage of this form of investment is that if the bank goes bankrupt, you will lose your gold or silver. Another problem is that if currencies collapse, there will likely be a shortage of gold and silver on the market and you might be forced to accept paper currency instead of your precious metals.

Diversification

The best way to store your bullion would be to diversify, just like you would with your investment portfolio. It's a good idea to have a little bullion in your home in the event of an emergency. However, you probably should consider storing the majority within secure vaults, like those offered by banks either through safety deposit boxes or allocated storage, or commercial bullion companies.

In fact, it might be an idea to split your investment up between the three types to

minimize your risks. If you have your gold and silver spread out over three or more vaults, if one bank or company becomes insolvent, you will still be able to easily access the remainder of your bullion.

But it's imperative that you do your research to make sure you are handing your bullion over to a company or financial institution that has a good reputation and is financially sound.

Conclusion

In the event of global currency collapse, gold and silver are the only things you will be able to count on to maintain their value. While you might think that complete devaluation of world currencies is impossible, remember

that nothing is impossible. You could wake up one morning to see that the dollar has crashed and isn't even worth the paper it's printed on.

For this reason, everyone should be prepared. One can't know how people will react when they discover their life savings have been erased and the money they have in their wallets isn't worth anything. That's why it's best to have something of value to trade and nothing is more valuable than gold or silver.

And by converting part of your savings into gold right now, you won't need to worry about being among those who will lose all their savings when currencies collapse. If you have all your savings in a deposit account then the first thing you need to do is convert part of it into gold and silver. Buy bullion coins or gold certificates or buy into a gold allocated account. Regardless of what

course of action you take, make sure you have access to physical gold because that's what will count. Stocks and other paper financial instruments will be useless but gold and silver bars or coins will rule.

Have You Read?

The Dividend Millionaire: Investing for Income and Winning in the Stock Market

The real key behind becoming a Dividend Millionaire is to adopt a long-term investing approach. You'll learn exactly how to turn your stock portfolio into an income producing investment.

This book and others are available in print at most online retailers.

Your capital is at risk when you invest in futures, stocks and commodities - you can lose some or all of your money, so never risk more than you can afford to lose. Always seek professional advice if you are unsure about the suitability of any investment. Past performance is not a reliable indicator of future results.

Printed in Great Britain
by Amazon